HONOLULU *HAWAII*

COOKING

with Betty Evans

HONOLULU *HAWAII*
COOKING

with Betty Evans

2-16-91
HONOLULU

Art by Gordon Evans

SUNFLOWER INK Palo Colorado Canyon, Carmel, Calif. 93923

ACKNOWLEDGEMENTS

Mahalo to Hal and Joan Clark for inviting us to Honolulu and sharing memorable dining experiences that led to the idea for this book. Mahalo to Ed and Marilyn Pollock and to Jim and Beverly Peck, kamaaina friends who have inspired us, and Ed and Ann Kitt for sharing a special Honolulu time with us, Madaline "Lindy" Boyes of the Hawaiian Visitors Bureau for her help, Steve Hoffmann for caring proofreading, M.F.K. Fisher (a cherished inspiration), and to our great friends Ric and Billie Masten for their encouragement and support over the years.

(paperback) 987654321

Library of Congress Catalogue No. 91-065920
ISBN 0-931104-33-5

❦ *iv* ❧

For Gordon

Aloha nui oe

HONOLULU
2·15·91

❧ vi ❧

THERE THEY ARE!

Situated 2500 air miles or so from San Francisco, the Hawaiian "mountains" rise from the ocean floor. Yes, they are mountains, breaking the blue Pacific as a string of ancient volcanoes. Some of them are still childlike in their constant bubbling and spewing of new land growth. All of the islands are very old, geologically speaking, and very new ecologically.

While there are many islands throughout our world with wonderful features, the climate, flowers, trees, surf, the almost unreal light in the islands, the cleanliness of the air, and the unending variety of foods of the cultural mix all seem to come to a focus in Hawaii!

Visiting a place is a completely different experience than day to day living. Joan, my dear wife of 42 years, and I have had nine superb years of being able to absorb this fascinating and cosmopolitan city. We have experienced this as "Haoles" (foreigners or non-locals) and as "malihinis" (strangers, newcomers). I mention this because sometimes tourists and local folk view things somewhat differently. However, the "Kamaainas" (long term residents) love everything about the islands that are their home as much as any two-week tourist.

We, and all of our special friends, like Betty and Gordon Evans, revel in sampling and sharing the fine foods and drink of this life. To be able to appreciate the fine art of food presentation, and its accompanying fine wine, seems to all of us to be one of God's great gifts!

While the other islands have many interesting restaurants, it is, in our opinion, Honolulu which has the most varied and comprehensive menus to offer. Honolulu is a world-class city, blessed by thoughtful and graceful architecture, a pleasant climate, abundant greenery and parks, and enough cultural diversity to pique anyone's curiosity. Yes, it is tourist-oriented, but this is not necessarily good or bad -- it just is!

The peoples of Hawaii are a true polyglot. All commingle, but still retain a cultural unity which produces a soft and beautiful society. The resultant foods are not always classic Chinese, Filipino or Japanese, but rather adaptations which make new taste treats. Classic foods of all the cultures are certainly available, but do try the local expressions.

Step outside on your hotel veranda at dusk, and soak up the light balmy breeze as you gaze on the horizon -- if you are lucky, you may see the "green flash" of the reflected light rays of the sun at the moment it drops into the deep blue ocean. It is okay to feel really good! You have been experiencing the magic of Hawaii - like no other place in this world of ours.

Aloha Nui Loa -

Hal Clark

HONOLULU
7-1-90

An arrival in Honolulu is always spectacular. The plane dips over the island of Oahu, and you can see the turquoise and indigo colors of the reefs and the long combers racing toward the shore. At the airport there is the scent of tropical plants. Trade winds drift through the open airport corridors. Everyone is dressed in casual flower print outfits, and people are smiling and hugging as they exchange fragrant flower leis. Honolulu is like no other city in the world. Visitors come to celebrate happy events -- weddings, birthdays, graduations, anniversaries and romantic honeymoons.

My husband and I first came to Honolulu to celebrate a wedding anniversary with friends who shared the same June nuptial date. They were living in Honolulu because our friend Hal had decided to leave his medical practice in Southern California and join the Navy. He was made a captain, and a new world of Navy and tropical medicine opened for him. When we arrived, Joan, his wife and my treasured special friend, was waiting for us with dazzling leis.

Joan took us to the Waioli tea room in the lush green Manoa Valley, where we had our first macadamia nut pie under a green ceiling of tropical trees. The Pali, a dramatic 1200-foot pass at the head of the Nuuani valley, was the day's next event. Winds were blowing and clouds sped by and from this great height we could look down across the valley to the Pacific.

From the Pali, we went to Barber's Point, where Joan and Hal were living. In their yard were tall coconut palms and yellow and white blooming plumeria trees. There was a thatched roof tropical hut where, after a swim in the warm clear sea, we had wine and watched the lights come on in Waikiki. The magic spell of this bit of paradise was cast for us that first day. We always want to keep returning.

Betty Evans
Hermosa Beach, California 1991

INTRODUCTION

A FEW NOTES ON HAWAIIAN FOOD AND COOKING

It is impossible to re-create some of the traditional foods of Hawaii in the average mainland kitchen, but any Honolulu cookbook would be remiss not to mention some of the unique treats that are available only on the islands.

The early Hawaiians did most of their cooking in an *imu*, which is a sort of underground oven. Special stones are heated to temperatures around 2000° F, then placed with the food, which has been covered with fragrant leaves. This is then covered with earth to keep the heat around the food. The men who do this imu cooking are very skilled and respected. It is still possible to taste succulent and marvelous food cooked in this ancient method at luaus done for special charities or family events.

Taro was brought to Hawaii around 450 A.D. and was the main staple food of the Hawaiian diet. Poi is made from the taro roots. Although there are many tourist jokes and jibes about its color and taste, poi is, in fact, a perfect foil for many of the salted dishes the locals enjoy. It is very nutritious, and at one time Hawaiians would each eat 10-14 pounds each day. There is one-finger poi, which is the thickest; two-finger poi (a little thinner), and three-finger poi, which is the thinnest. Poi is eaten with the fingers from lovely wooden poi bowls that are handed down in the family for generations. When you are visiting the museum, along with the antique poi bowls you will see special oblong bowls for serving poi dogs. These were a special breed of three-toed dogs fattened on a diet of poi.

Opihi are small limpets that cling to the rocks in the sea. To collect them is very dangerous because of swift tides and fast currents. Drownings are common, so opihi catching is not recommended for tourists. If you eat them in Honolulu, let someone else do the catching.

Limu is seaweed. There are at least 40 varieties eaten in Honolulu. On certain beaches you can watch local people collecting them in shallow waters. They are not always too popular with tourists, but are a traditional food.

I have not included the Portuguese doughnut "Malasadas" in this book, because for really good Malasadas you need a huge pot of bubbling oil. There are many variations on the recipe for them in Honolulu. Many celebrities offer their recipes and participate in the cooking for island fairs and fund raising events. Look for these events and enjoy the taste of a Malasadas, hot and fresh from the pot.Laulau is seasoned pork and fish with taro, steamed in ti leaves. You can find them at the Willows restaurant and sometimes on Aloha Friday menus. They are quite good, and though some recipes say you can substitute spinach leaves, corn husks, or foil for the taro leaves, it just will not taste right. So enjoy them in Honolulu.

Spam must be mentioned. Hawaii uses nearly four times more Spam than any other state, so don't be surprised if a piece of fried Spam is included on your breakfast or lunch plate.

Shave ice can only taste perfect when it is purchased from a Waikiki shave ice stand. The ice is "shaved" and then drizzled with your choice of sweet multicolored syrups. The next step is to walk along the beach licking your shave ice. This is fun.

Tall graceful coconut palms sway with the trade winds. These trees provide not only coconuts for food, but leaf and bark materials for clothing and shelter.

On the mainland, coconuts are available at most supermarkets. Choose one that you can hear the coconut liquid swishing around inside when you shake it. The scientific name, "cocos nucifera," is derived from the Portuguese word for monkey's face. You can see, with a little imagination, that the three "eyes" do look like a face. To prepare a coconut, pierce these "eyes" with an icepick. Drain the liquid into a bowl. It may be drunk or used in a sauce.

Crack the coconut open with a hammer. It helps to wrap the coconut in a towel so the pieces stay in one place. Sometimes the coconut is placed in a 350° oven to help the coconut meat pull away from the shell, but I find that this tends to dry out the meat, which you do not want. Peel away the brown skin with a vegetable parer or sharp knife. The coconut meat pieces can now be grated by hand or by processor or blender.

Coconut milk can be made by heating one cup of regular milk with one cup of water. Pour over the grated coconut and let stand 30 minutes. Strain through a strainer or double thickness of cheesecloth. You must press down hard to extract the liquid. This will yield 2-3 cups of milk. Refrigerate. Be sure to stir before using, and do not heat at a high temperature or it will curdle.

Coconut milk can also be made from dried coconut. Place two cups of dried coconut in a bowl. Heat two and a half cups of regular milk, pour over the coconut, and let stand for 30 minutes. Proceed as with fresh coconut. This milk is a little sweeter. If you are in a hurry, canned coconut milk can be used with quite good results.

In Honolulu you will find that food is often served garnished with orchids and a spirit of Aloha!

TABLE OF CONTENTS

HONOLULU

HAU TREE LANAI
2-18-91
HONOLULU

1. PUPUS - APPETIZERS

PARK
HONOLULU
2-18-91

ONO J AND J SOY CHICKEN WINGS

Ono is the Hawaiian word for "good" or "delicious," and that is just what these chicken wings are. Bring out a platter of these tasty appetizers and watch them disappear. They are addictive! A big plus for this recipe is that they are marinated and baked all in the same pan.

> *4 lbs chicken wings*
> *1 cup soy sauce*
> *1 cup brown sugar*
> *1/2 cup butter*
> *1 tsp hot or Dijon-type mustard*
> *3/4 cup water*

Cut each chicken wing at the joint to make two pieces. Discard the tips. Combine remaining ingredients, and heat in a saucepan until the butter is melted. Stir and remove from flame. Arrange the chicken wings in a shallow baking pan. When the sauce is cool, pour over the wings and mix for an even coating. Refrigerate and marinate overnight or at least four hours. Give the wings a stir during the marination for better flavor absorption.

Place the pan in a 350° oven. Bake for 45 minutes, stirring now and then. Drain and serve either hot or cold. Garnish with lime slices, fresh cilantro or diced pineapple.

PAPAYA WITH PROSCIUTTO

Honolulu has taken a classic Italian appetizer and substituted papaya for the traditional melon. It is a tantalizing combination. Prosciutto may be purchased at any Italian store and in many supermarket deli sections. Sliced firm mango may also be used for this appetizer.

> *1 ripe papaya*
> *6 slices of thinly-sliced prosciutto*
> *freshly-ground pepper (optional)*

Peel the papaya, remove the seeds, and slice it lengthwise into about 1/3-inch slices. Arrange the slices in an attractive pattern on a plate. With scissors, cut the prosciutto slices to gracefully drape across the papaya. Sprinkle with a few grinds of fresh pepper if desired. Papaya seeds may be dried and used as pepper in your pepper mill; their flavor adds a tropical touch. This will serve four.

ISLAND RUMAKI

Rumaki is said to have its origin with the Japanese of Honolulu. It may be cooked over a low bed of charcoal, on a hibachi, or in your oven.

The quantity of ingredients will depend on how many you need to serve. For each serving:

> *1/2 strip of bacon*
> *1/2 of a chicken liver*
> *1/2 water chestnut*
> *1 square (about 1"x1") of pineapple or papaya*
> *a sprinkling of soy sauce*

Sprinkle the liver with soy sauce. Wrap the liver and chestnut in the bacon strip. Securely hold in place with a toothpick or small bamboo skewer. Top with the pineapple piece. Place on a metal rack over a pan (to catch the drippings) in a 400° oven, until the bacon is crisp (about 15-20 minutes). If you use a hibachi, turn the skewer while cooking so each side is cooked evenly.

2-19-91
HONOLULU

LOMI LOMI SALMON

You may wonder about the origin of this traditional Honolulu appetizer, as salmon is not a fish found in tropical waters. In the 1800's, Hawaiians worked on ships that traveled to America's Northwest coast. They developed a strong liking for the salted salmon of this area, and soon they were bringing kegs of salmon back to Hawaii. It was mixed with tomato and onion, and massaged together with the fingers. Lomi lomi means "massage" in Hawaiian.

> *1/2 lb fresh or salted salmon*
> *for fresh salmon: juice of 2 lemons or limes, plus 1 T salt*
> *4 green onions, minced*
> *2 large or 3 medium tomatoes, peeled and diced*
> *1/2 cup crushed ice*

If the salmon is fresh, remove skin and bones. Cut into little pieces and cover with the citrus juices and salt. Place in the refrigerator to marinate for 4-6 hours, then drain the marinade.

If the salmon is salted, cover with water to soften for 6 hours. Drain, remove skin and bones, and shred.

Mix the salmon with the tomatoes and onions. With clean fingers, "lomi lomi" until the mixture is blended but retains a little texture. Chill for one hour. Just before serving, mix in the crushed ice.

You can serve lomi lomi on a bed of shredded lettuce, or in a seashell. Often in Honolulu it is served simply in small paper cups. This will make 8 little appetizers. The salmon belly is the preferred cut used by locals.

2-15-91
HONOLULU

THAILAND AVOCADO APPETIZER

Honolulu is one of the best places in the Pacific to sample the tantalizing flavors of Thai cuisine. Avocados grow well in the island climate, and are plentiful for this popular dip.

2 ripe avocados
2 T fresh lime juice
1 T fresh cilantro, minced
1 red pepper, peeled, roasted and finely diced
    (can be found prepared in jars)
1/2 medium red onion, finely chopped
salt and pepper to taste
dash of hot sauce or Tabasco

Peel the avocados and mash with a fork to medium crumbly texture. Add remaining ingredients and blend together. Serve with potato chips or shrimp crackers (kroe poeck).

HAWAIIAN BEEF JERKY (Pipikaula)

The first cattle were brought to the Islands in 1793 by Captain Vancouver as a gift to King Kamehameha, and ranching soon became an important industry. In the early ranch days, the cattle were wild and tough. The paniolo (Hawaiian cowboy) found that a good way to use this beef was to make jerky. There are many methods used, such as drying under screens in the hot sun. The seasonings will always include soy sauce and garlic.

This updated recipe will work well no matter where you live. These tasty little morsels are great served on a pretty green leaf as an appetizer nibble.

> *1 lb flank steak*
> *1/3 cup soy sauce*
> *1/4 cup sherry*
> *1/4 cup brown sugar*
> *1 clove of garlic, minced*
> *1 T fresh grated ginger (optional)*
> *1/2 tsp crushed dried hot red pepper (optional)*

Cut the flank steak in four equal pieces. Mix the remaining ingredients in a bowl. Place the steak pieces in the bowl and stir so that each piece is covered with the marinade. Place in the refrigerator overnight or for at least 8 hours.

Heat the oven to 200°. Remove the meat from the marinade, place on a rack over a shallow pan (to catch the drips), and bake for 5 hours. Remove, cool, and cut into bite-sized strips. Store in the refrigerator in an airtight glass jar. This recipe may be doubled. In earlier times the jerky was not refrigerated, but this method does ensure even temperature for longer-lasting jerky.

HONOLULU 6·10·90

PACIFIC RUMAKI SPREAD

This is an alternate version of rumaki that can be made ahead of time. I first tasted this at a dinner party in Honolulu. It was served by a lovely Hawaiian hostess on a terrace overlooking Diamond Head, as a prelude to an island dinner party. The water chestnuts add interesting texture to the spread. Serve with shrimp chips or sesame crackers.

1 lb fresh chicken livers, cut in half
1/2 cup sweet butter
1 small onion, minced
dash of cayenne pepper or hot pepper sauce
6 slices of bacon, cooked and crumbled
1 8-oz can of water chestnuts,
    drained and coarsely chopped
salt and pepper to taste
3 T soy sauce

Melt the butter and saute the livers and onion until the onion is limp and the livers slightly pink. (Overcooking liver will make it tough.) Mash with a fork, or use a blender or food processor, to make a smooth mixture. Add remaining ingredients and blend well. Place in a pretty bowl and refrigerate. This spread may be garnished with a few fresh cilantro leaves.

2-15-91
HONOLULU

2-18-91
WILLOWS
HONOLULU

2. SOUPS

PORTUGUESE BEAN SOUP

There must be as many versions of this popular Honolulu soup as there are varieties of hibiscus on the city's streets. Local politicians, musicians and schoolteachers swear by their family recipes, and often cook and sell bean soup for charity fund raisers. Basically, it is a bean soup, brought from Portugal by the first Portuguese immigrants. It combines beans, ham hocks and cabbage in a thick tasty soup. One might call it a "minestrone" of the Islands, meaning that this and that can be added to a basic recipe.

> *1 lb dried small red or kidney beans*
>   *(or a combination of both)*
> *1 medium onion, sliced*
> *2 ham hocks*
> *salt and pepper to taste*
> *1 8-oz can of tomato sauce*
> *2 stalks of celery, diced*
> *2 medium-sized potatoes, peeled and diced*
> *1 small cabbage, chopped or thinly sliced*
> *1/2 cup uncooked small elbow macaroni*
> *1/2 lb Portuguese or any hot style sausage, thinly sliced*

Cover beans with water and soak overnight. Drain and place beans in a soup pot. Cover with 2 quarts of water. Add onion, ham hocks, salt and pepper. Cover and simmer for one hour, stirring now and then.

Remove cover and take out the ham hocks. Add tomato sauce and celery. Remove ham from the bones and dice. Return to the pot and simmer, uncovered, for 20 minutes. Add remaining ingredients and continue to cook for an additional 30 minutes. If the soup is too thick for your taste, thin with water or white wine. Garnish with minced parsley or watercress. This will serve 6-8.

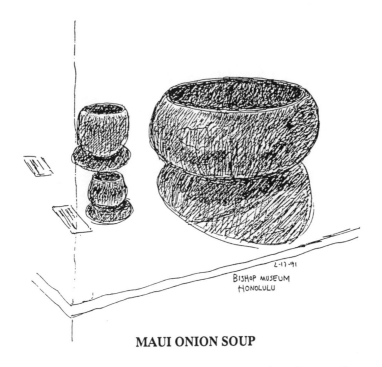

2-17-91

BISHOP MUSEUM
HONOLULU

MAUI ONION SOUP

Maui onions have a reputation for sweetness and tenderness. Some Honolulu residents eat them peeled and raw like an apple. It is no wonder that soups using these special onions are very popular.

4 T butter
2 T peanut or sesame oil
6 medium-sized Maui onions or other sweet onion,
    peeled and thinly sliced
salt and pepper to taste
1 T flour
2 quarts chicken broth (may be homemade or canned)
1 cup dry white wine
soy sauce for garnish

Heat the butter and oil in a soup pot. Add the sliced onions. Over a low flame, stir around until onions are limp. Cover and cook for 15 minutes, giving a stir now and then. Uncover. Stir in the salt, pepper and flour. Add the broth and wine. Simmer over a low flame, uncovered, for 40 minutes.

This will serve 6. Add a few drops of soy sauce to each bowl for a little Hawaiian touch.

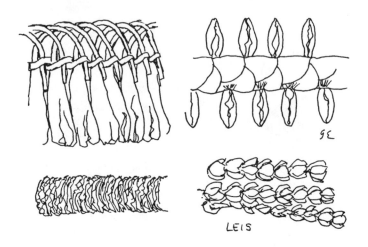

LEIS

SENEGALESE SUMMER SOUP

It is not only immigrants from Asia who have added to the recipe variety of Honolulu. Another important contribution comes from the various military groups that have been stationed in Hawaii, who enjoy entertaining and making friends.

This cool refreshing soup is popular at summer parties in Honolulu. Its pale yellow color and mixture of exotic flavors are a taste pleasure.

1 cup minced or finely shredded cooked chicken breast
2 cups chicken broth (homemade or canned)
1 cup half and half or light cream
2 T flour
2 T butter
1 T curry powder
egg yolks
salt and pepper to taste
toasted chopped peanuts and chives for garnish

Melt the butter. Add the flour and curry powder, and blend. Slowly add broth. Cook and stir until slightly thickened.

Mix the cream or half and half with the egg yolks. Gently add to the broth and cook over a low flame for one minute. Stir in the chicken. Season to taste with salt and pepper. Refrigerate for 4 hours or overnight before serving.

This will serve 4. Garnish with the peanuts and a few snips of chives. If it is a cold stormy day, this soup may be served hot.

ISLAND FISH CHOWDER

There does not seem to be any place in the world that can compare to Hawaii in its diversity of blended food flavors. Each immigrant brought foods from another country to the Islands, and before long they were all mixed and mingled into a unique cuisine.

The missionaries from New England brought chowders that were perfect for the cold winters back home. It does seem hard to imagine that in a tropical land they still continued to make chowder. Their food supplies from New England included salt pork, potatoes and dried cod. Even though fresh fish was very plentiful, they preferred dried cod from "home." Today, however, in Honolulu freshly caught fish is used and sometimes even soy sauce is added to the chowder.

> 1 T peanut oil
> 1/4 lb salt pork or bacon, cut in 1/2-inch dice
> 1 large onion, peeled and sliced
> 4-5 potatoes, peeled and diced (4 cups approximately)
> 3/4 lb fresh boneless fish (snapper, cod, etc),
>   cut in 1-1/2" squares
> 2 cups water
> 1/4 cup white wine
> salt and pepper to taste
> 2 cups half and half

Heat the oil in a soup pot and add the salt pork or bacon. Stir and cook until golden brown. Remove from pan with a slotted spoon and set aside. Add onion and saute until just limp. Add potatoes and swirl around to coat with pan drippings. Add water, wine, salt and pepper. Cover and cook until the potatoes are tender but not mushy. Return salt pork or bacon to the pot, along with the fish and half and half. Simmer uncovered, stirring until the fish is cooked just to firm. The time will depend on the fish (usually 5-8 minutes will be enough). Garnish with a few snips of fresh parsley. This will serve 4-5.

HONOLULU
6·30·90

WATERCRESS SOUP

A morning visit to the Honolulu Chinatown market is a food adventure. The shoppers are wise and experienced. They know just how to pick the best and freshest of all the tempting foods for sale. In this market you can find some of the most beautiful watercress in the world. Long-stemmed, with perky green leaves, it is used for stir-fries and this tasty nutritious soup.

You can still see the watercress fields on the outskirts of the city. Some have been lost to development, but there is a determined effort to preserve these historical cress lands.

> *4 cups chicken broth (homemade or canned)*
> *salt and pepper to taste*
> *2 tsp soy sauce*
> *1/2 lb boneless pork, cut into thin strips or tiny cubes*
> *1 T minced ginger*
> *1 bunch of watercress*
> *2 eggs (optional)*

In a soup pot, combine the broth, pork and seasonings. Cover and simmer for 20 minutes over a low flame. Wash the watercress and lay on a board. Cut the bunch into 1/2" pieces. Add the stems to the broth and cook one minute, then add the leaves and cook an additional minute. Some cooks like to add two beaten eggs to the soup at the last minute. This will make two large bowls.

BISHOP MUSEUM
HONOLULU

3. SEAFOOD

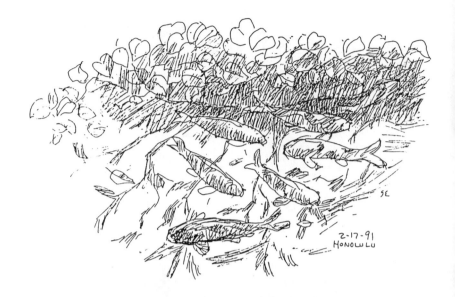

2-17-91
HONOLULU

BAKED OPAKAPAKA IN ORANGE CITRUS SAUCE

Opakapaka is a sort of snapper family fish that is abundant in Hawaiian waters and very popular with Honolulu diners. On the mainland you can substitute red snapper (also known as rockfish). Baking fish is a healthy and easy method of cooking. Serve with hot steamed rice.

> *1 lb Opakapaka (or red snapper) filets*
> *1/4 cup fresh orange juice*
> *1 tsp grated orange rind*
> *1 T soy sauce*
> *1 T sesame oil*
> *2 T minced green onion tops*
> *salt and pepper to taste*

Combine all the ingredients except fish in a shallow baking dish large enough to fit the fish in one single layer. Stir with fork to blend. Add the fish and cover with the marinade. Place in a cool place in the kitchen for one hour.

Heat oven to 400°. Place the pan in the oven, uncovered, for 10 minutes or until the fish is cooked. Baste once with the sauce while cooking. Be careful not to overcook. To serve, place the fish with the sauce on warmed plates. You may wish to add a few orange slices for a garnish. This will serve 2. This dish is also good served chilled for hot-weather dining.

2-18-91
HONOLULU

AIEA SHRIMPS WITH BASIL BUTTER

On the porch of our friend's condo in the hills overlooking Pearl Harbor, there is a huge pot of basil. I was amazed at the large size and fullness of the plant. It seems basil thrives in the Honolulu climate. We sat drinking wine as we watched the sunset over the Pacific, and then were served this superb basil-flavored shrimp.

1 lb large raw shrimp, peeled and deveined
4 T butter at room temperature
1 T fresh basil, finely cut
juice of one medium lemon
1 tsp chopped parsley
salt and pepper to taste
2 T olive oil

In a bowl, blend the butter, basil, lemon juice and parsley. Heat the olive oil in a frying pan. Over medium heat, cook the shrimp just until pink. Add the butter mixture and stir to combine flavors. Add salt and pepper to taste. Garnish with a few sprigs of fresh basil. This will make two generous servings.

❧ 17 ❧

HONOLULU 6·29·90

BROILED AHI WITH LIME CILANTRO SAUCE

Ahi is a deep water fish, known to mainlanders as yellowfin tuna. Hawaiian chiefs enjoyed the adventure of fishing for this large fish in the deep waters off Honolulu. Ahi seems to have a special sea tang to its flavor and has always been a very favorite island fish. In former days it was eaten raw or preserved by salting. Today it is marinated and broiled with a light sauce. This treatment with lime and cilantro is popular.

> *1 lb Ahi filets*
> *2 T soy sauce*
> *2 T peanut oil*
> *juice of one lime*
> *1 T fresh minced cilantro*
> *1 tsp grated fresh ginger*
> *salt and pepper to taste*

Try to purchase two equal-sized pieces of fish. Mix the soy sauce and oil in a shallow glass bowl. Marinate the fish for 1-2 hours, turning once in the marinade. Place the fish with the marinade on a double thickness of aluminum foil, turning the sides of the foil up slightly to retain the marinade. Blend remaining ingredients. Broil the fish, basting with the lime mixture, until cooked. Remove fish from foil and pour remaining juices over the fish. This may be served garnished with a lime wedge and a few fresh cilantro leaves, and will serve two.

PARTY SHRIMP CURRY

Honolulu parties often have curry as a main dish. Pale pink shrimp in a coconut-accented sauce, surrounded with pretty bowls of condiments, is impressive. The host or hostess can prepare the dinner ahead of time and with only a few last-minute touches it will be ready for guests.

> 1 lb medium raw shrimp, peeled and deveined
> 6 T butter (1/3 cup)
> 1 medium-sized onion, finely chopped
> 1/3 cup flour
> 2-3 T curry powder
> 2 T fresh grated ginger (or 1 T dry ginger)
> 2 cups milk
> 1 cup canned or fresh coconut milk
> salt to taste
> dash of Cayenne pepper (optional)

Melt the butter in a large saucepan. Cook onion just until limp (do not brown). Add the flour, ginger and curry. Stir over a low flame to blend. Gradually add the regular and coconut milk, stirring until the mixture is smooth. Add shrimp, with salt to taste, and the Cayenne if used. Cook over a low flame just until shrimp turns pink. This will take about five minutes. At this point the curry may be refrigerated until party time.

The condiments for the curry might include chopped peanuts or macadamia nuts, minced green onions, finely diced cucumbers, chutneys and grated coconut. Curry is served with plenty of hot steamed rice. A dish of sliced fresh tropical fruits is often added to the festive table. Individual portions of curry may be served in papaya shells. This will serve 4, and can be increased for large parties.

HONOLULU 7-1-90

BAKED MACADAMIA NUT MAHI-MAHI

Mahi-mahi is a tropical saltwater fish. Sometimes it is called dolphin fish, but it is not in any way related to the dolphin, which is an intelligent mammal. You will see this fish on every menu in Honolulu, and it is prepared in many ways. It is especially delicious in this easy recipe with the flavorful macadamia-nut topping.

1 lb mahi-mahi (2 filets)
2 T butter
2 T fresh lemon juice
2 T dry white wine
salt and pepper to taste
1/4 cup macadamia nuts

Melt the butter and add lemon, wine, salt and pepper. Place the two filets in a glass oven dish. Cover with the sauce. Swish around to make sure the sauce is evenly distributed. Cover the dish with foil. Bake at 350° until the fish is cooked (about 20 minutes).

To prepare the nuts, chop them coarsely, place in a pie pan, and bake until light brown. This may be done in the same oven with the fish. The nuts brown quickly (about 8 minutes), so keep your eye on them. When light brown, remove from the oven.

To serve, place the mahi-mahi on two warmed dinner plates. Divide the remaining sauce between them. Top with the nuts and serve at once to two.

2·15·91
HONOLULU

4. POULTRY

CHICKEN LUAU

Luau is the Hawaiian name for taro leaves. This staple plant of the Islands is not easily obtainable outside the islands, so spinach is usually substituted on the mainland. In Italy, poultry recipes with chicken are called "Florentine," so one might say this is the Hawaiian version of this classic combination. A short baking in this recipe version is more convenient than the usual stewing and produces a more attractive result.

3 to 3-1/2 lb chicken, cut up, or chicken parts
flour for dusting
2 T butter plus 1 T oil
salt and pepper to taste
1 cup coconut milk (fresh, canned,
    or made from dry coconut - see Hawaiian foods)
2 bunches spinach or fresh taro leaves
    (or 2 10-oz pkgs frozen chopped spinach, drained)
grated coconut for garnish

In a stew or soup pot, heat the butter and oil. Dust the chicken with flour. Lightly brown in the pot. You have to do this in two batches, so add more oil and butter if needed. Season with salt and pepper and cover with water (about 4 cups). Cover the pot and cook over a low flame until the chicken is tender.

Wash the spinach or taro well. Cook, covered, in a pot, with just the water that is left clinging to the leaves, until they are limp and tender. Do not overcook. Drain and chop coarsely. Mix with 3/4 cup of the coconut milk, reserving the remaining 1/4 cup.

Place the spinach or taro mixture in a buttered dish. With a slotted spoon, remove the chicken parts from the broth. Place the pieces on the spinach. Spoon 1 cup of the broth over the chicken, topping with remaining coconut milk. Bake in a 350° oven, uncovered, for 20 minutes. Garnish with grated coconut. This will serve 4. Chicken breasts cut in quarters work well for this casserole.

CORNISH GAME HENS
WITH TROPICAL FRUIT GARNISH

Cornish game hens make a most attractive dish for a special party. They are easy to make and quite impressive. In this recipe, the hens are first marinated in a soy-ginger sauce. They are then roasted and garnished with your choice of tropical fruits before serving.

> *2 Cornish game hens*
> *1/4 cup peanut or sesame oil, or a mixture of both*
> *1/2 cup soy sauce*
> *1/4 cup sherry*
> *2-3 T fresh minced ginger*
> *2 cloves garlic, finely minced*
> *tropical fruit for garnish*

You will usually find, inside the hens, a little packet containing the liver, neck and gizzard. Remove these "insides." They may be discarded or used in soup. Rinse inside of hens and drain. Mix the soy sauce, sherry, ginger and garlic. Place the hens in a bowl and cover with the marinade. Refrigerate and marinate for several hours or overnight, turning now and then so the marinade covers all parts of the hens.

Drain the marinade from the hens and reserve. Place the hens on a rack in a roasting pan. If desired, an onion or orange may be placed in the cavity for extra flavor. Tie the legs together. Brush with the marinade. Bake at 375° for one hour, basting occasionally. To serve, remove from the pan and untie strings. Serve each person a half or whole hen, depending on the appetites. For the garnish, mix fresh pineapple, papaya or mango cut in small dice, and spoon on top of the hens. Another garnish often used in Honolulu is lime juice mixed with minced fresh cilantro leaves, and some lime wedges.

2-15-91

LEMON CHICKEN

Chinese in origin, lemon chicken is popular in Honolulu because of the abundant local lemon crop. Serve lemon chicken with lots of steamed rice.

1 lb boned chicken breast
juice from one fresh lemon, strained
1 T soy sauce
1 T sesame oil
1 T minced ginger
oil for frying (peanut preferred)

LEMON SAUCE:
juice from one fresh lemon, strained (1/4 cup)
1/2 cup chicken broth
1 T cornstarch
2 T sugar

Cut the chicken into 1"x1" pieces. Blend lemon juice, ginger, soy sauce and sesame oil. Add chicken and marinate at least one hour.

Prepare lemon sauce by mixing ingredients in a small saucepan. Make sure the cornstarch is mixed well, so the sauce will not be lumpy. Cook over a low flame, stirring as it cooks, to make a smooth sauce. When it is thickened set aside.

In a wok or frying pan, heat about 1/2 inch of oil. Fry the chicken pieces, stirring so they are evenly cooked. Remove from the pan to heated serving plates. Warm the sauce and spoon over the top. This can be garnished with fresh lemon slices, and will serve 2.

CHICKEN WITH LONG RICE

When I first tasted this comforting dish, it gave me the same feeling as eating Jewish chicken soup. You instantly feel healthy and well. This soupy Island combination is found in most Honolulu restaurants on Fridays, a day when men and women dress in Aloha clothes (flowered shirts and dresses) and the menus feature favorite Hawaiian food.

There are variations to this dish; the size of the chicken parts can vary, along with the seasonings. One can add extra touches like soy sauce or fresh cilantro. This is the basic recipe.

> *1 3-lb chicken, whole*
> *1 T (or more) minced ginger*
> *1 onion, finely chopped*
> *salt and pepper to taste*
> *4 oz long rice (rice noodles)*
> *minced green onions for garnish*

Place the chicken in a large soup pot. Cover with water. Add ginger, onion, salt and pepper. Cover and simmer until the chicken is tender, about 50 minutes. Remove chicken from liquid. Place the long rice in the liquid and soak for 20 minutes. Cool chicken slightly for easier handling, and de-bone. Cut the chicken into large chunks and return to liquid. Skim off excess fat from the top. Bring to a simmer and cook an additional 10 minutes, until the long rice is tender and the liquid is reduced. Some cooks break the long rice in half before soaking, but I like the longer strands. This is best served in shallow bowls. Use a slotted spoon to serve so each portion has an equal amount of long rice with some liquid. Garnish with green onions to serve four.

CHICKEN PINEAPPLE CURRY

Curry is on the menus of many Honolulu restaurants. It is definitely very popular and each chef seems to have his or her own flourish and special creative touch. This combination of curry and fresh island pineapple is one of the more tasty island curries.

2 T peanut oil, or other salad oil
1 medium apple, cored and peeled
1 green pepper, topped and seeded
1 T fresh grated ginger
2 medium onions
3 T flour
1 T curry powder (more if desired)
1-1/2 cups chicken broth
1/2 tsp salt
1/2 cup white wine
1 lime (juice and grated rind)
2 cups cooked cubed chicken
1 cup fresh pineapple cubes
(or one 8-1/2 oz can pineapple chunks)
fresh cilantro for garnish

Chop the apple, green pepper and onions together. Add the ginger. Heat the oil in a large deep pot. Fry the onion mixture until just limp. Mix in the flour and curry, and stir around to blend. Add the broth, wine and salt, and simmer, uncovered, for 15 minutes, stirring now and then so you have a well-mixed base. Add the chicken and simmer another 10 minutes. Lastly, add the pineapple and lime. Cook an additional 5 minutes.

This curry is served on top of hot steamed rice garnished with cilantro leaves. To accompany the curry, condiments such as chopped peanuts, chutney, minced green onions, grated coconut, and crumbled cooked bacon are added to the table in individual bowls. This will serve four.

CHICKEN WITH EGG ON RICE
(Okako Donburi)

The Japanese were among the first immigrants to arrive in Hawaii. They came in 1868 to work in the sugar cane fields. They brought their traditional Japanese food, which today has merged and mingled with the Island cuisine. The name of this lovely recipe means "mother and child" because it contains both the chicken and the egg. It is a popular picnic dish. Each portion is packed in a pretty lacquer box.

2 whole chicken breasts
salt and pepper to taste
4 green onions
1 cup chicken broth
1/4 cup soy sauce
1/4 cup sake or dry sherry
1 cup mushrooms, thinly sliced (optional)
6 cups hot cooked rice

Place the breasts in a saucepan and cover with water. Add salt and pepper to taste. Cover and simmer until tender (about 30 minutes). Cool in the broth. Remove chicken and discard bones and skin. Slice in thin slivers. This may be done ahead.

To assemble the dish, heat one cup of the broth the chicken was cooked in. Add soy sauce, sherry or sake, and mushrooms. Simmer a few minutes to blend flavors. Cut the onions in one-inch lengths and add to the broth with the chicken.

Divide rice into four bowls. Lightly mix the eggs and pour gently into the hot broth. Stir for a minute for the eggs to cook. Ladle the mixture over the rice, scooping from the bottom so each portion has an even amount of everything. This will serve four.

2·18·91
HONOLULU

2-14-91

BISHOP HONOLULU
MUSEUM

5. MEATS

TERIYAKI STEAK ISLAND STYLE

Every menu in Honolulu has some kind of teriyaki dish. Teriyaki is part of life in Honolulu. The name comes from a Japanese word -- teri is charcoal, and yaki is broil. There seem to be many variations of the teriyaki sauce. In Honolulu, fresh ginger and sugar are added to give an extra zip and a little shiny glaze. This recipe can also be used with poultry or fish.

> 2 lbs top sirloin steak (or 2 lbs of boneless fish or poultry)
> 1/4 cup soy sauce
> 2 T sherry or sake
> 1 T crushed fresh ginger
> 1 clove of garlic, minced
> 2 T brown sugar
> 2 T sesame oil
> 1 tsp grated orange or tangerine rind (optional)

Mix the sauce ingredients together. Cut the steak into four serving pieces and place in a flat dish. Pour the sauce over the meat and stir around so each piece is coated. Marinate at least 4 hours, or overnight if desired. The meat may also be cut in cubes and skewered.

To cook, remove from sauce and place under a broiler. Cook to desired doneness, turning once. The steak may also be cooked over charcoal. Dribble remaining sauce over meat before cooking. This will serve four. A few lime slices make an attractive garnish.

HAWAIIAN STYLE PORK CHOPS

Pineapple and pork make a tantalizing flavor combination. This recipe is easy and quick (in Hawaiian, they say "wiki wiki" for quick). These chops may be served with sweet potatoes or rice.

1 T peanut or other oil
4 loin or rib pork chops
1/2 cup pineapple juice
3/4 cup dry white wine
1 T soy sauce
2 slices of pineapple, medium diced
1/2 tsp salt
1 tsp cornstarch
cilantro leaves for garnish (optional)

Heat the oil in a frying pan large enough to hold four chops. Brown the meat on both sides. Remove and set aside. Mix the juice, wine, soy sauce and salt together. Add to the pan, stirring and blending with any remaining pan juices.

Return the pork to the pan along with the pineapple. Cook over a medium flame, uncovered, until the sauce is thickened and the meat cooked through. This will serve two hungry people. Garnish with a few fresh cilantro leaves if desired.

CHINATOWN SWEET AND SOUR PORK

The first Chinese came to Honolulu in 1852 as contracted labor to work in the sugar plantations. From this humble beginning the Chinese were able to save money. Within ten years they owned 60% of the stores in downtown Honolulu, which became Chinatown. Even the devastating fires of 1900 didn't stop them. Chinatown was rebuilt and rebuilt again. In past years much remodeling of this and that has gone on, but fortunately much of the flavor of old Honolulu still remains.

1 lb boneless pork
2 T soy sauce
1 T sherry
2 T flour
2 T cornstarch
1 green pepper, cut in strips
1 onion, peeled and sliced
1 cup pineapple chunks (fresh or canned)
peanut or other oil for frying

SAUCE:
1 T soy sauce
1/2 cup white wine or cider vinegar
1/4 cup brown sugar
2 T ketchup
1 cup pineapple juice
2 T cornstarch

Cut the pork in bite-sized pieces (3/4"x3/4"). Combine soy sauce, sherry, flour and cornstarch in a bowl. Mix with a fork until smooth. Dredge the pork cubes in this mixture so all parts of the meat are coated. Heat enough oil in a frying pan (non-stick works well) or wok to cover bottom about 1/4" deep. Over a medium flame, fry the pork pieces until golden brown and cooked. Remove with a slotted spoon to a warm platter. Adding more oil if necessary, stir-fry the green pepper and onion until limp. Add the pineapple. Blend the sauce ingredients together to make a smooth sauce. Add to the pan and cook, stirring until the sauce thickens. Add the pork and stir until it is blended with the rest of the ingredients. Taste for seasoning; you may need a dash of salt. Serve to two on warmed plates with rice.

POLYNESIAN STYLE BRISKET

Polynesian flavors seem to blend perfectly in this brisket recipe. This is a wonderful dinner for company, as it cooks without any fuss in the oven. It may even be made a day ahead. This method of cooking with a foil cover keeps all the flavorful juices captured inside the pan. Just be sure to carefully tuck the foil around the pan so you retain a sealed cover without any breaks. You might want to double the recipe and have an extra brisket for a picnic. It is marvelous cold.

> *1 4-5 lb beef brisket*
> *1 cup soy sauce*
> *1/2 cup dry sherry*
> *1/2 cup brown sugar*
> *1 cup orange, lemon or pineapple juice*
> *2 cloves of garlic, peeled and minced*
> *salt and pepper to taste*
> *2 T freshly grated ginger (or 1 T dried ginger)*
> *1 cup fresh or canned pineapple, diced, for garnish*

Place the brisket in a bowl or shallow pan. Mix together remaining ingredients and pour over the brisket. Make sure all parts of the meat are covered. Refrigerate at least 4 hours, or preferably overnight.

Place the brisket in a baking pan with the marinade. Cover tightly with a double layer of foil. Bake at 325° for 3-1/2 hours. Check during the baking to make sure there is enough liquid; if not, add extra soy sauce or fruit juice, being sure to replace the foil tightly.

To serve, remove meat from juices. Slice and serve with warmed pan juices and pineapple on top. This will serve 4-5. In Honolulu, rice is usually served with the brisket.

U.S
ARMY MUSEUM
2-17-91
HONOLULU

KOREAN STUFFED FRIED GREEN PEPPERS

The Korean immigration to Hawaii began in 1903. Like most of the ethnic groups, they came to work in the cane fields. From these difficult beginnings, they have achieved financial success and today hold many high positions in the government and business world. Korean cooking has blended into the melting pot of Honolulu cuisine. This treatment of green peppers is zesty and tasty, a good dish for any time.

> *3 green bell peppers*
> *1 lb lean ground beef*
> *1/2 tsp pepper*
> *1 T sesame oil*
> *1-2 garlic cloves, peeled and minced*
> *2 T soy sauce, plus some extra for sprinkling*
> *flour for breading*
> *1 egg, beaten*
> *1/4 cup peanut or vegetable oil*
> *1/2 of an 8-oz can whole water chestnuts*

Wash the peppers and cut in half lengthwise. Remove seeds and membranes. Mix beef with sesame oil, garlic, pepper and soy sauce. Chop the water chestnuts coarsely and add to the beef mixture. Fill the peppers with the meat mixture. Dredge each pepper all over in flour, then dip in beaten egg.

Heat the oil in a frying pan. Fry the peppers slowly over a low flame, turning now and then, for 30 minutes. Serve with additional soy sauce sprinkled on the top, and hot steamed rice. This will serve 2-3.

JOAN'S MALAYSIAN SATAY

Satays are part of the intriguing Pacific rim cuisine. In Honolulu, satays made with a small amount of meat or poultry on a skewer are sometimes served as an appetizer. Other times, as in the portions for this recipe, they are perfect for dinner with hot steamed rice and a cucumber salad. This is an authentic version collected in Penang by my special friend Joan.

1 lb boneless beef (flank or top sirloin)
(chicken breast may also be used)
1 T sugar
4 entire green onions, chopped
2 T curry powder
1 clove garlic, minced

Cut the meat into small bite-sized pieces. Combine the remaining ingredients in a bowl. Mix and add a little water to make a paste. Marinate the meat in this mixture for one to two hours. Thread in skewers and either broil or barbecue until of desired doneness. Serve with the following sauce:

MALAYSIAN PEANUT DUNKING SAUCE
3/4 cup Spanish peanuts, salted or unsalted
4 T lemon juice
2 T molasses (or 2 T brown sugar)
1 tsp dried chili peppers (or 1 tsp chili powder)
1 tsp grated fresh ginger
1/2 cup soy sauce
1 cup water
2 garlic cloves, minced

Chop peanuts finely. Combine with remaining ingredients in a saucepan. Simmer 15 minutes over a low flame. Serve sauce in individual bowls; dunk the satay in the sauce.

If this is served for dinner, rice and cucumbers are a traditional addition. For dinner, this will serve two; as an appetizer it will serve four.

MARITIME MUSEUM

2-15-91
HONOLULU

BEEF AND PINEAPPLE ON A SKEWER

Marinated steak cubes combined with pineapple make a delightful dinner. The combination of flavors is typical of Pacific cuisine. This recipe can be enlarged for a party and cooked on an outside barbecue.

1 lb top sirloin steak, or other tender steak
1/4 cup soy sauce
2 T brown sugar
1 clove of garlic, finely minced
1 tsp freshly grated ginger
1 T peanut or sesame oil
1 cup fresh pineapple, cut in cubes,
    or one can (8-1/4 oz) cubes, drained

Cut the beef in bite-sized cubes (about 3/4"x3/4"). Mix the remaining ingredients, except pineapple. Marinate the beef overnight, or for at least an hour. Remove from marinade and reserve marinade. Thread meat on skewers, alternating with pineapple cubes. Broil or barbecue until meat is desired doneness. Baste with reserved marinade while cooking. Serve with hot rice and garnish with a small orchid, if available. This will serve two.

TOMATO PEPPER BEEF

Its origin is Chinese, but with Hawaiian touches this easy one-pan dinner dish is always flavorful and fun to make. Serve with lots of hot steamed rice.

> *1 lb flank, sirloin or other tender steak*
> *1 T soy sauce*
> *1 T sherry or sake*
> *2 T peanut or other vegetable oil*
> *2 medium tomatoes*
> *1 green bell pepper*
>
> SAUCE
> *1 tsp grated fresh ginger (optional)*
> *2 T ketchup*
> *1 T cornstarch*
> *2 T soy sauce*
> *3/4 cup water*
> *minced green onions for garnish*

Cut the meat into 2"x1/2" strips, or into small bite-sized pieces. Mix the soy sauce and sherry or sake in a bowl. Add the meat and marinate for at least an hour.

Cut each tomato into 8 wedges. Seed the pepper and cut into thin strips. Mix the remaining ingredients together in a bowl and blend well.

In a frying pan, heat the oil. Brown the meat quickly, and while still rare in the center, remove and set aside. Add the green peppers to the pan and stir around. Now add the blended sauce mixture. Stir around in the pan. Add the meat and tomatoes (and ginger if used). Cook and stir just until the tomatoes are hot. The idea of this recipe is to have the tomatoes and green peppers firm. Garnish with minced green onions and serve to two.

BISHOPE MVSEVM
HONOLULU
2-17-91

KALUA PIG

Kalua pig is the grand star of a Honolulu luau. The ancient traditional way of preparing Kalua pig is to use an imu, which is a sort of underground oven. The men who prepare the food for luaus are experts who know just the right moment to remove the pig so it is tender and succulent on the inside and crispy on the outside.

One should not miss a luau adventure. Even though they may be tourist-oriented, the food (served buffet-style) is always delicious, and the accompanying ceremonies quite moving.

Because cooking in an imu is not possible for everyone, the islanders, who never tire of nibbling on Kalua pig, have developed an easy oven method for making this local favorite.

> *4-5 lbs boneless pork butt*
> *2-3 T rock or kosher salt*
> *1/3 cup Wrights (or other brand) liquid smoke*

Score the pork on both sides to 1/2" depth. Rub well with salt and liquid smoke on all sides. Wrap in a double thickness of foil, sealing securely. Place on a rack in an oven roasting pan, and bake at 325° for 4 hours. Sweet potatoes mixed with bananas may be placed in foil and baked separately the last hour and a half.

To serve, remove from foil and place the "pig" on green leaves. Shred the meat with two forks and serve at once. This will serve four.

HONOLULU
7-2-90

6. VEGETABLES

BAKED GINGERED PAPAYA

Papaya is a refreshing addition to any dining occasion. With its pale lovely color, it not only looks pretty, but has a most pleasant taste when baked.

> 2 firm ripe papayas
> 4 T butter
> 2 T fresh lime or orange juice
> 1 T freshly grated ginger
> sprinkling of Cayenne pepper (optional)

Cut the papayas in half lengthwise, and remove the seeds. Melt the butter with the fruit juice and ginger. Arrange the papaya halves in a buttered baking pan. Spoon the butter mixture into the little cavities of the papayas. Bake at 300° for 20 minutes. Just before serving, a sprinkling of Cayenne pepper may be added, if desired.

KIM CHI (Pickled Cabbage)

Korean winters are long and fiercely cold. To help them survive these grey and frosty times, Koreans pickle huge amounts of vegetables, seasoned with lots of garlic and hot peppers so that one will feel warm inside. In Honolulu everyone eats kim chi as an accompaniment to almost any food. Usually it is served in small bowls. It is quite easy to make in your own kitchen.

> 1 medium-sized cabbage
>   or one medium Bok Choy cabbage
> 1 qt water, mixed with 1/2 cup salt
> 3 entire green onions
> 2 cloves garlic, minced
> 1 tsp salt
> 1 T dry red pepper (use less if you want it medium hot)
> 1 T minced fresh ginger
> 2 T sugar
> water to cover

Core and cut the cabbage into one-inch squares (it can also be shredded). Place in a bowl, cover with the saltwater mixture, and place a weight on top. The idea is that this slightly wilts the cabbage for the next step. Let this mixture remain in the bowl for 2 hours, stirring now and then.

Drain and rinse the cabbage. Add the remaining ingredients and mix well with the cabbage in a stainless or glass bowl. Cover with a plate, with a weight on top to keep the cabbage pressed down. Let this stand at room temperature for several days, giving it a little stir each day. It will smell strong and that is the way it should. When it tastes right to you, place in the refrigerator and keep covered. It may be put in jars for convenience. Celery or cucumbers can also be used as separate pickled vegetables, or added to the cabbage bowl.

2·15·91
HONOLULU

PAN FRIED HAWAIIAN CABBAGE WITH PORK

Cabbage is always in demand in Honolulu kitchens. Sometimes a bit of leftover Kalua pig or pork roast is used in place of fresh pork. Portuguese sausage can also be used; simply cut the sausage in 1/4" slices for a spicy creation.

> *2 T peanut or vegetable oil*
> *1/2 cup fresh pork, cut in thin strips or tiny pieces*
> *1 clove garlic, minced*
> *1 small head of cabbage*
> *1-2 T soy sauce*

Heat the oil in a frying pan. Lightly brown the pork and garlic. Shred the cabbage. You should have 4-5 cups. Add with the soy sauce, salt and pepper to the pan. Stir to blend. Cover the pan and cook over a low flame until the cabbage is tender but not mushy. Give the dish a stir now and then during the cooking. The Filipinos like to add a cup of chopped tomatoes to the cabbage during the last few minutes of cooking.

HONOLULU
2-16-91

PINEAPPLE IN A CASSEROLE

Although a pineapple is a tropical fruit, in this recipe it is an accompaniment to a main dish, and will take the place of a vegetable side dish. It is especially nice served with poultry main dishes.

> *1/4 cup (4 oz) butter (room temperature)*
> *3/4 cup sugar*
> *4 eggs*
> *1 20-oz can crushed pineapple, drained*
> *1-1/2 tsp fresh lemon juice*
> *1/2 tsp curry powder*
> *1 tsp freshly grated ginger (or 1/2 tsp dry ginger)*
> *3 cups cubed white bread (crusts removed)*
>   *(about 6 slices)*

Cream butter with sugar until smooth. Add eggs one at a time, beating well after adding each egg. Carefully stir in the pineapple. Blend in lemon juice and seasoning. Fold in the bread. Place in a buttered 1-1/2 quart baking dish. Bake at 350° for 50 minutes, until the top is golden brown. This will make four servings.

AIRPORT
HONOLULU 7-2-90

CHINESE STIR-FRIED ASPARAGUS

The Chinese who came to Hawaii were from the Canton region of China. They were masters of stir-frying, a method of cooking developed because of the shortage of fuel in China. Meals could be cooked quickly by stir-frying everything together in a wok. If you do not have a wok, a frying pan can be used.

> *1 lb medium-sized asparagus*
> *2 T peanut, sesame or other cooking oil*
> *salt and pepper to taste*
> *2 T soy sauce*

Take each stalk in your hand and bend. It will naturally snap off between the tender upper half and the bottom woody stem. The bottom stems may be used for soup. Lay the top stems on a cutting board, and cut them into 1-inch pieces on a diagonal.

Heat the oil to a medium heat in a wok or frying pan. Add the asparagus pieces and sprinkle with salt and pepper. Give a stir and cover. Shake the pan a few times while the asparagus is cooking. After two minutes, lift the lid and stir the stems around. Cover and repeat the procedure for another three minutes. Uncover, and add the soy sauce. Give a final stir. Of course this may be all cooked uncovered (stir-frying for 5 minutes), but by covering, you create a little steam, which makes the asparagus tender inside and crunchy outside. This will serve two.

SHORE BIRD

OAHU SWEET POTATOES

A traditional food of the Hawaiians, sweet potatoes are nutritious and delicious. This recipe version includes fresh island fruits. You may want to remember this treatment of sweet potatoes, with its refreshing flavor combinations, for Thanksgiving.

4 medium-sized sweet potatoes (or yams)
1 orange, sliced
1 lemon, sliced
2 slices of fresh or canned pineapple, diced
1/4 cup rum or other liquid
butter
1/2 cup brown sugar
a few slivered macadamia nuts (optional)

Cook the potatoes in water to cover until tender (about 35 minutes). Remove, and when cool enough to handle, peel and cut into 1/4" slices.

Butter a baking dish. Place half the potato slices in a layer. Divide the fruits in half. Layer half of the fruit on top of the potatoes. Add the remaining half of the potato slices, then the remaining half of the fruit. Bake, covered, for 20 minutes at 350°. Remove cover and sprinkle top with brown sugar and dots of butter. Bake an additional 10 minutes. Garnish with slivered nuts if used. This will serve 4-5.

2-16-91
HONOLULU

2-16-91
SHORE CAFE
HONOLULU

7. SALADS

KAPIOLANI PARK PICNIC SUMI SALAD

Kapiolani Park is a favorite spot for local picnics and relaxation. This 170-acre park, dedicated to the people of Honolulu in 1877 by King Kalakaua, was named after his wife. It is a park where one can easily spend the entire day watching all the various activities, and there are plenty of tables for enjoying a picnic. A sumi salad is perfect for a Kapiolani Park picnic.

1 small head of cabbage, chopped rather finely
5 whole green onions finely sliced
1 3-oz package chicken ramen, broken in pieces
2 cups cooked and chilled chicken
    (breast works well), shredded
1 cup coarsely chopped roasted almonds
2 T sesame seeds lightly toasted in 1 T oil,
    or toasted slivered almonds

DRESSING
The flavor packet from the ramen
1/2 cup peanut oil
2 T sesame oil
3 T white wine or rice vinegar
2 T sugar
salt and pepper to taste

Combine salad ingredients in a bowl. Mix the dressing together and blend well with a fork or whisk. Add to the bowl and toss well. This will serve eight. Garnish with a few fresh cilantro leaves or some minced green onion.

SUNSET PAPAYA SALAD

Sunsets are spectacular in Honolulu, and it is easy to arrange to be in a special place to watch them. One of the best places to be is on a dinner cruise in the waters off Honolulu. You can stand on the deck, sipping your favorite beverage, and watch the sky show.

This salad is lovely and refreshing with tropical flavor.

> *1-1/2 cups red leaf or butter lettuce, washed*
> *1 medium-sized papaya, chilled*
> *1/2 cup salted peanuts*
> *   or roasted macadamia nuts, coarsely chopped*
> *3 T peanut or salad oil*
> *2 T rice vinegar*
> *salt and pepper to taste*

Tear the lettuce into bite-sized pieces. Peel the papaya and remove the seeds. Cut into small cubes. Blend the oil, vinegar, salt and pepper. Place the papaya and lettuce in a bowl. Pour the dressing over and mix lightly. Sprinkle the nuts over the salad. Serve at once to four.

CUCUMBER NAMASU SALAD

Namasu is a cool and invigorating Japanese salad, and a favorite "kama'aina" recipe. The use of lemon or lime juice adds a zesty taste.

> 1 large cucumber
> 2 T salt
> 1/3 cup lime or lemon juice
> 2 tsp sugar
> 1/2 tsp grated fresh ginger
> 1 small carrot, peeled, topped and grated

Peel the cucumber and cut in half. Slice into 1/4" slices. Mix with the salt and let stand for 15 minutes. Drain and pat dry. Mix the remaining ingredients in a salad bowl. Add the cucumbers and toss lightly. Sometimes a small drained can of baby clams is added to this salad. This will serve four.

TROPICAL CHICKEN SALAD

A salad made with this hint of a tropical taste combination is always a winner, and a perfect menu choice for a picnic or summer party. Banana bread is a nice accompaniment for this refreshing salad.

> 2 cups cooked and diced chicken breast
> 1 can (8-1/4 oz) pineapple chunks,
>   or 1 cup fresh pineapple chunks
> 1 cup trimmed celery, cut into small dice
> 1/4 cup macadamia nuts or peanuts, coarsely chopped
> 1 tsp curry powder
> salt and pepper to taste
> 1/4 cup mayonnaise

Combine all the ingredients in a bowl. Mix together and refrigerate. This may be made the day ahead, and can be garnished with fresh cilantro leaves. This salad will serve four.

PAPAYA AND AVOCADO SALAD WITH PAPAYA SEED DRESSING

A papaya is a sort of miracle fruit. Every bit can be used. When you peel the papaya, save the peelings and rub them on your skin. They will feel cool and give your pores vitamin A. Remove the seeds and spread on a plate to dry. Papaya seeds have a light pepper taste and can be used ground on foods or in this salad dressing. If you wish to make this salad heartier, simply add cooked shrimp, chicken, or cooked crab. A little watercress can also be mixed into the salad.

1 ripe papaya
2 ripe avocados
butter lettuce

PAPAYA SEED DRESSING
1/2 tsp dry mustard
1/4 cup sugar
1 tsp salt
1 cup salad oil
1/2 cup white wine or rice vinegar
1 T fresh lime or lemon juice
2-3 T white, red or green onion, chopped
2 T papaya seeds

Peel and slice the papaya and avocado. Arrange on four plates on top of butter lettuce leaves.

Put all the dressing ingredients, except the papaya seeds, in a blender. Blend to mix. Add the seeds and continue blending just until they are the size of coarse ground pepper. Spoon over the salads to serve 5. This will make a little over two cups of dressing, so you should have leftover dressing for another salad. This dressing is nice with fruit salads.

OUTRIGGER REEF
2-15-91
HONOLULU

8. HONOLULU BREADS AND DRINKS

PORTUGUESE SWEET BREAD (Pao Doce)

Around 1878, Portuguese sailors began leaving their whaling ships while they were docked in Hawaiian ports. Life in the Islands seemed more pleasant than the hard, never-ending toil of whaling. In the years that followed, nearly 13,000 Portuguese came to the Islands as part of a labor recruitment plan. Many became foremen on the plantations. They brought with them a small four-stringed guitar-like instrument. The sound of this "Braguinho" delighted the islanders. One of the more famous players, Edward Purvis, was as agile and quick as a jumping flea, and the instrument became known in the local dialect as "uke-lele," which means jumping flea.

The Portuguese ladies brought recipes from home, among them the sweet bread which is now found everywhere in Honolulu. The famous King's bakery even exports it to the mainland. Recipes vary, and some are for huge quantities. This is a manageable version and will make a lovely light bread which is especially good toasted with butter and jam.

1/2 cup lukewarm water, plus 1 T sugar
2-1/4 packages of dry yeast
4 oz. (1/2 cup) sweet butter, at room temperature
1/2 cup warm milk
1 cup sugar
4 eggs
1 T salt
grated rind of one lemon
4 to 5 cups flour

Place the water and the 1 T sugar in a large bowl. Add the yeast and stir. Cut the butter into several pieces, for easier melting, and add it to the warm milk. Add the cup of sugar and stir to blend. Now add this to the yeast mixture. Stir so all ingredients are well mixed.

Take 3 of the eggs and mix lightly with a fork. Add to the yeast mixture, with the salt and lemon rind. Next add the flour, one cup at a time, blending in with a wooden spoon or your hands. You will feel when the dough is stiff enough after this flour addition. If you feel it needs a little more body, add some more flour. The dough should be soft but not runny. Turn out the dough on a floured board and knead until the dough is smooth. This will take 5-10 minutes. Gather the dough up to make a large ball and place in a lightly buttered bowl. Cover with a damp towel and let rise in a warm spot until it is doubled in size.

Punch down the dough. Divide in half and shape into round balls. Place in either two 9-inch buttered cake pans, or two buttered 9-inch iron frying pans. Cover again with a dampened towel. Let rise until doubled. Mix the remaining egg well, and brush the tops of the bread with it. Bake at 350° for 30 minutes or until the top is a dark golden brown. Cool on racks.

ROYAL HAWAIIAN
HONOLULU

BANANA NUT BREAD

There are plenty of banana legends in Hawaii. When King Kalakaua died in San Francisco, his body was placed in a coffin for his final voyage to Hawaii for burial. In Hawaii he was moved to another coffin, and a banana stalk was placed in the first coffin and buried in the Kawaiaho churchyard. It was believed that if this had not been done the coffin would have called out for a relative to die to fill the empty coffin. It is still believed that to dream of a hole in the ground means that your open grave is waiting for you. To change this vision, the dreamer must go out and plant some part of a banana tree.

There are not any curious legends about banana bread in the Islands; it is just good, and popular in every kitchen. This easy recipe has macadamia nuts added for a local touch.

> *1/3 cup butter or shortening, at room temperature*
> *2/3 cup white sugar*
> *1 tsp grated orange or lemon rind*
> *2 eggs*
> *1-3/4 cups white flour*
> *1/4 tsp baking soda*
> *1/2 tsp salt*
> *2 tsp baking powder*
> *1 cup mashed banana (about 2 medium)*
> *1 T rum (optional)*
> *1/2 cup chopped macadamias or walnuts*

Cream the shortening, rind and sugar together. Add the eggs, one at a time, beating well after each addition. Sift the dry ingredients and add alternately with the bananas and rum to make a smooth mixture. Fold in the nuts

Grease a 9x5x3" loaf pan. Place the bread batter in the pan and bake at 350° for one hour until golden brown.

BUS STOP 2-14-91
HONOLULU

PINEAPPLE CORN MUFFINS

I have often enjoyed a cup of steaming Kona coffee with a muffin at various outdoor terraces along Waikiki. There always seems to be a wide choice of types of muffins with Island jams. Muffins are a legacy of missionary kitchens, but have been improved with Hawaiian flavors. This combination with pineapple and corn meal is one of the best.

1 cup flour
1/4 cup sugar
3 tsp baking powder
1 tsp salt
1 cup corn meal or bran
1/4 cup shortening or butter (room temperature)
1 egg, beaten
1/2 cup milk
1 cup drained crushed pineapple, canned or fresh

Sift flour, sugar, baking powder and salt together. Stir in corn meal or bran. Blend in the shortening with a fork or your fingertips to make a crumbly mixture. Add egg, milk and pineapple and stir to blend. Place in muffin cups or a well-greased muffin pan. Bake at 425° for 15-20 minutes until golden brown. This will make about 2 dozen muffins.

TROPICAL GINGER BREAD

Fresh ginger is used in many island dishes. Fresh gingerroot is the root of a ginger plant. Sometimes it is called a hand, because when it is harvested the shape (with a little imagination) looks like a hand. When you select ginger, make sure it is firm and smooth. Don't be afraid to break off a small piece from the "hand." It is best to buy just what you need at the time. This easy bread will be ginger scented and is lovely with tea or for dessert with fresh tropical fruits.

> *1 cup buttermilk*
> *3-4 T peeled, grated fresh gingerroot*
> *1/4 cup vegetable or peanut oil*
> *1 egg*
> *grated rind of one lemon*
> *1/2 tsp salt*
> *2-1/2 cups all-purpose flour*
> *2/3 cup sugar*
> *1 tsp baking soda*
> *1 tsp baking powder*
> *1/2 tsp cinnamon*
> *a pinch of ground cloves*

Combine the buttermilk, grated ginger, oil, egg, lemon rind and salt. Mix lightly until everything is well blended.

Sift the remaining dry ingredients into a bowl. Make a well in the center of this mixture. Stir the buttermilk mixture into the well and stir all together just until you have a smooth mixture. Do not overmix.

Grease and flour a 9x5x3" loaf pan. Place the dough in the pan and bake at 350° for one hour and ten minutes. Cool on a wire rack for 5 minutes and remove from pan.

ISLAND DRINKS

Sitting on a shaded terrace overlooking Waikiki Beach and watching lovely young ladies in long flowered dresses carrying trays of tropical drinks is an Island experience. These are just some of the many choices offered in Honolulu.

CHI CHI

1/2 cup pineapple juice
2 T coconut syrup
2 oz vodka

Combine ingredients in a cocktail shaker; shake well and pour over crushed ice in a 14-oz. glass to make one chi chi.

HONOLULU SUNSET COOLER PUNCH;
(Non-alcoholic)

1 cup orange juice
1/2 cup lemon juice
1 cup pineapple juice, unsweetened
1 bottle (1 liter) ginger ale
ice cubes
mint sprigs for garnish

Combine all ingredients in a bowl. Garnish with a few mint sprigs. This will serve 4, but the recipe may be doubled, tripled etc. for larger groups.

MIKE'S KILLER MAI TAI

Mike Purpus is a world-famous surfer and has spent time in the Islands participating in surfing competitions. This is his original mai tai recipe.

1 jigger of white rum
2 oz. orange juice
2 oz. pineapple juice
1-1/2 oz. coconut syrup
1 jigger "151" strong dark rum
1/2 oz. cherry-flavored brandy
splash of grenadine syrup

Mix white rum, juices, and coconut syrup together. Fill a 10- or 12-oz tulip glass with crushed ice. Pour the rum/juice mixture over the ice. Add the jigger of "151" on top. Float the cherry-flavored brandy on top, with a splash of grenadine. This will make one drink.

PINA COLADA

3 oz. white rum
3 T coconut milk
3 T crushed pineapple
2 cups crushed ice

In a blender place the rum, coconut milk, pineapple and ice. Blend at high speed until smooth. Garnish with a pineapple slice and serve with a straw. This will make one drink.

WAIKIKI FROZEN PINEAPPLE DAIQUIRI

1-1/2 oz. white rum
4 medium-sized pineapple chunks (around 1/4 cup)
1 T lime juice
1 cup crushed ice

Combine all ingredients in a blender. Blend at low speed until the mixture is smooth. Serve in a champagne glass. This makes one drink.

BLUE HAWAII

1-1/2 ozs. light rum
1-1/2 ozs. pineapple juice
1 oz. blue Curacao
2 T lemon juice
small cube of fresh pineapple
1/2 cup crushed ice

In a blender place all the ingredients and blend until smooth. This will make one drink.

2-17-91
HONOLULU

ACADEMY OF ARTS
HONOLULU

2-17-91
HONOLULU

9. DESSERTS

HAUPIA (COCONUT PUDDING)

Every true Hawaiian luau will offer these pretty, translucent squares of pure coconut delight. Many recipes use fresh coconut milk, but I have found that canned coconut milk produces an easy and authentic haupia. It is the custom to place the pudding on top of a ti leaf, but a citrus leaf can also be used.

1 can (14 oz) coconut milk
5 T sugar
5 T cornstarch
3/4 cup water

Pour the coconut milk into a saucepan. Mix the sugar and cornstarch together in a bowl. Stir in the water to make a smooth blend. Add to coconut milk and cook over a low heat, stirring until the mixture thickens. This will take about 6-8 minutes. Pour into an 8 or 9-inch square pan. Refrigerate until firm. To serve, cut into 2-inch squares. Another variation on this recipe is to serve it on top of sliced papaya or pineapple. This will make 16 squares of haupia.

PACIFIC COCONUT KISSES

These delicate morsels melt in your mouth. They are the ideal addition to a fresh fruit or sherbet dessert plate.

2 egg whites
1/2 cup sugar
1-1/2 cups shredded coconut
shortening to grease baking sheet

With an electric mixer or whisk, beat the egg whites until stiff. Gently fold in the sugar and coconut until all the ingredients are blended.

Grease 2 cookie sheets well. Drop the dough from a teaspoon onto the sheets to make little kisses. Bake at 275° until very pale brown - about 45 minutes. Let sit on the baking sheet one minute, then remove to a cookie rack. Cool completely and store in an airtight container. This will make a little over two dozen kisses.

WAIKIKI COCONUT CREAM PIE

A pie that looks like a lovely mound of delectable coconut goodness and melts in your mouth. This is what this star of Honolulu desserts is all about. Any desired pie crust may be used; I prefer a basic graham cracker crust. Remember, whichever crust you decide to use, do not add the filling too soon or the crust will become soggy. You only need enough time for chilling; about two hours ahead is perfect.

> *1 9" pie crust, baked and cooled*
> *2/3 cup sugar*
> *2 cups milk*
> *3 egg yolks, beaten*
> *3 T cornstarch*
> *1 tsp vanilla*
> *2 T butter*
> *1 cup grated coconut (fresh is best)*
> *1 cup whipping cream (8 oz)*
> *2 T sugar for whipped cream*
> *5 T additional grated coconut for topping*

In a one-quart saucepan, combine the sugar and milk. Heat over medium heat. Mix the cornstarch with the egg yolks. When the milk mixture is hot, remove about 1/4 cup and blend with the egg yolks. Stir until smooth, then add slowly to the rest of the milk mixture. Cook over a low flame for 3 minutes, stirring. Remove from heat and add vanilla, butter and coconut. Stir until the butter is melted. Cool and pour into pie shell.

Just before serving time, whip the cream with the sugar until stiff. Carefully spoon over the pie. Top with grated coconut. This will make 8 servings.

PINEAPPLE UPSIDE-DOWN CAKE

It is fun to bake this popular island cake in an iron frying pan. You will be amazed at the superior baking qualities of iron pans. If you do not own an iron frying pan, rush to your local hardware or kitchen store and buy one! They last forever and have many handy uses.

1/2 cup butter
1 cup brown sugar
4 fresh or canned pineapple slices (reserve juice)
1 cup pecan
* or other nuts - halved macadamia nuts are nice*
3 eggs, separated
1 cup sugar
5 T pineapple juice
1 cup flour
1 tsp baking powder
1 tsp grated fresh ginger (optional)

Melt butter over low flame in a 10-1/2 inch iron skillet. Add brown sugar and stir to make an even coat in the pan. Remove from heat and arrange the pineapple rings and nuts in an attractive design. Sometimes a few maraschino cherries are used in the design.

Beat the egg yolks, sugar and pineapple juice. Sift flour and baking powder, and add to batter. Pour carefully over the pineapple-brown sugar mixture. Bake 50 minutes at 350°. Remove from oven and place on a metal rack for 10-15 minutes. Run a knife around the edge to loosen the cake. Place a plate on top of the frying pan and turn upside down. This cake is best served slightly warm. It may be topped with whipped cream if desired. This cake may also be baked in an 8x8 pan, but it isn't quite the same.

JUDY'S MACADAMIA NUT BARS

These easy-to-make cookies are some of the most addictively delicious morsels you can imagine. Macadamia nuts give a taste of Hawaiian crunch and flavor. This recipe, from a special family friend, is a winner.

BUTTER CRUST
1 cup flour
1/4 cup sugar
1/2 cup butter

FILLING
2 eggs
1 tsp vanilla
1-1/4 cups brown sugar
2 T flour
1/4 tsp salt
1/4 tsp baking powder
1/2 cup flaked coconut
1 cup (or 1 3-1/2 oz can) toasted macadamia nuts,
    coarsely chopped
powdered sugar for topping

To make the crust, blend the butter, sugar and flour together with a fork to make a crumbly texture. Press into a nine-inch square pan. Bake at 350° for 20 minutes or until light brown. Remove from the oven.

For the filling, beat the eggs, vanilla and brown sugar together until smooth. Sift the flour with the baking powder and salt; stir into the egg mixture and blend well. Fold in the nuts and coconut to complete the filling.

Gently spread the filling over the crust. Bake an additional 25 minutes at 350°. Remove from oven and place on a rack. Sprinkle with powdered sugar. Cool 5 minutes, then cut with a knife into desired size squares. For a romantic dessert, serve with chilled champagne!

HONOLULU
2-15-91

TROPICAL AMBROSIA

There are few places in the world with the abundance of fresh fruits in their cuisine that Honolulu has. They are used for garnishes, added to main dishes, or often just sliced and served on a glossy green ti leaf. Sometimes they are simply mixed together in a pretty bowl and topped with a few sprigs of mint or a tiny orchid. Ambrosia means "food of the gods."

2 large oranges
3 bananas
2-1/2 cups pineapple cubes
1 cup sliced papaya or mango (optional)
1-1/2 cup shredded coconut (fresh or packaged)
1 cup powdered sugar

Peel the oranges; discard the seeds and cut into thin slices. Peel and slice bananas. Place in a bowl and add pineapple. Sprinkle in the powdered sugar and coconut, and give a light toss. Garnish with mint leaves and, if available, an orchid. Serve to 4. Some chefs add a splash of white rum to the ambrosia.

HEAVENLY COCONUT CAKE

A light and delectable cake, layered with fresh grated coconut and whipping cream, is a taste of paradise. This is a cake for special occasions, and is often served at Honolulu weddings.

> *2 cups flour*
> *1 tsp baking powder*
> *1/8 tsp salt*
> *8 eggs, separated*
> *2 cups sugar*
> *1 tsp vanilla*
> *1/4 cup fresh lime or lemon juice, strained*
> *1 T finely grated lemon or lime peel*
> *for cake pans: 2 T butter at room temperature,*
> *   plus 2 T flour*

> FILLING
> *1/4 pint (8-oz carton) whipping cream*
> *1-1/2 cup freshly grated (or packaged) coconut*

Sift the flour, salt and baking powder together. Place the egg yolks in a mixer bowl. Mix at medium speed, adding sugar gradually, until thick and lemon-colored. This will take 4-5 minutes. Add the fruit juice, peel and vanilla. Gradually add the flour mixture, blending well after each addition. In another bowl, beat the egg whites at high speed until they are stiff. With a rubber or plastic spatula, fold the whites into the egg yolk mixture, blending gently until well mixed.

Coat three 9-inch cake pans with the butter. Flour each pan so there is an even layer of flour. Pour in the batter and bake at 350° for 25 minutes. The top and sides should be golden brown. Cool in pans for 5 minutes, then loosen with a knife. Turn out on a cake rack to cool.

To make the filling, simply whip the cream until stiff. Fold in the coconut and frost the top and sides of the cake with this mixture. Keep refrigerated until serving time. This will make 10 large slices.

BISHOP MUSEUM
2-17-91

HONOLULU SIGHTS

ABC DISCOUNT STORES
29 locations in Waikiki

Everyone forgets their toothpaste or something during last minute vacation packing. This is the quick and easy place to pick up needed things. With coupons from free tourist guides you can purchase macadamia nuts or other touristy things at a discount.

ALA MOANA CENTER
Ala Moana and Kapiolani Blvds

With 180 shops on three levels, this is like a gigantic *souk*, which 45 million shoppers visit each year. There is every type of store from first-class to small curio shops. The Makai Market food court is an adventure in casual dining.

ALOHA TOWER
Pier 9, adjacent to Irwin Park and Nimitz Hwy, 537-9260

This 184-foot tower was built in 1921 to welcome visitors and returning residents to Hawaii. Ride the elevator for a panoramic view from Diamond Head to the Waianae mountain range.

BISHOP MUSEUM AND PLANETARIUM

1525 Bernice St, 847-3511, closed Mondays.

The Bishop Museum houses the world's greatest collection of Pacific anthropology and natural history of the Islands. Among the famous artifacts is the blazing red headdress and cloak (made with a half-million feathers of the rare Mamo bird) of King Kamehameha. There are fierce idols and models of outrigger canoes. Shop Pacifica offers beautiful reproductions of museum pieces and an excellent selection of contemporary docent tours. The Bishop is not to be missed.

CHINATOWN

King, Nu'uanu and Beretania Streets

Still surviving after two disastrous fires and years of political turmoil, this is a colorful area with moods of old Honolulu. The open air markets and lively food stores along the street are an adventure. It is possible to buy excellent take-out food for picnics or hotel room dining. There are old-style lei stands and a colorful array of busy shoppers. Tours of this historic area are given by the Chamber of Commerce.

FOSTER BOTANIC GARDEN

50 N Vineyard, 533-3214

Twenty acres of rare tropical plants fill this quiet oasis. There are 4000 species of flora. The plants are labeled and the gift shop can arrange for them to be brought to the mainland.

HAWAII MARITIME CENTER

Pier 7, 536-6373

The Maritime Center Museum is modeled after King David Kalakaua's boathouse, which used to stand near this spot. The boathouse was a place for the king to entertain and also was used for various water sports. It was this king who brought canoeing, surfing, barge racing and even the hula back into the Hawaiian culture. Within this most exciting museum are relics from the ocean and marine history displays. Children will be fascinated with an exhibit of Hokulea voyages. You can board two historic sailing ships. The *Falls of Clyde* is the only four-masted square-rigged ship still in existence. Another treasure of the museum is a humpback whale skeleton. The Pier 7 Gift Shop in the museum will have just the nautical gift you are looking for.

HONOLULU ACADEMY OF THE ARTS
900 S Beretania St,
538-1006, closed Mondays

This must be one of the most beautiful art museums in the world. Galleries open out into pleasant garden courts. Fresh flower arrangements are everywhere. The art collection is outstanding. There is not only one of the finest collections of Asian art, but many fine French Impressionist paintings as well. The gift store is a terrific spot to buy unique presents. Try not to miss lunch at the Garden Cafe.

HAWAII STATE CAPITOL BLDG, S Beretania,
Punchbowl and Richards Sts, 548-2211

The impressive winged-style Capitol building is open to visitors, and is well worth a stop. The Capitol reflects the spirit of the state with koa wood paneling, volcanic rock and lovely reflecting pools. There is a statue of Father Damien in front of the Beretania entrance.

HONOLULU ZOO
151 Kapahulu Ave, 923-7723

If you enjoy tropical birds, this zoo is for you. It is small and charming. Recently there has been a renovation going on so the zoo will continue to improve. A local art show hangs on the zoo fences on the weekend.

IOLANI PALACE
King and Richards Sts, 522-0832 (Tour Information)

Iolani means "Heavenly Hawk." This is the only "royal" palace in the United States. It was completed in 1882 by King Kalakaua and was used for a residence and lavish parties. This king was called "the merry monarch" because of his fondness for the good life. Following his death, the palace was used as a seat of government. After nine years of work and a cost of over seven million dollars, the marvelous restoration is now finished. Tours are given by reservation only. This palace was the first in the world to have flush toilets and one of the first to be lit with electricity.

INTERNATIONAL MARKET PLACE
2330 Kalakaua Ave

High rise development threatens to do away with this rather old-fashioned group of little tourist shops with its old Banyan tree. This market is always colorful and lively. There are places to buy food and dine while you are entertained by local musicians.

KAPIOLANI PARK

This was Hawaii's first public park, and has been enjoyed by millions since its dedication in 1877. There are 300 acres with lots of shade under Kiawe and Banyan trees. Every kind of sport from tennis, jogging and archery to kite flying goes on here. Visit the park on a Sunday and enjoy watching local residents picnic. The Kodak Hula Show is enjoyed by tourists on Tuesdays, Wednesdays and Thursdays. On Sundays there are band concerts. This park has absolutely everything.

KAWAIAHAO CHURCH AND KING LUNALILO'S TOMB

957 Punchbowl St, 538-6267

This church, completed in 1842, contains 14,000 coral blocks. It is called "the Westminster Abbey of Hawaii." Inside the church on the upper balcony are portraits of Hawaiian royalty. The pipe organ has 2,500 pipes and a most impressive sound. Sunday services are in Hawaiian and English.

Honolulu 6-19-90

MISSION HOUSES MUSEUM

553 S. King St, 531-0481, closed Mondays

The mission houses look like a bit of New England in the middle of Honolulu, and this is the way it was. On Saturdays a living history program is given, where volunteers dressed in clothing of the time discuss life in 1831. The museum shop features Hawaiian handcrafts, including quilt patterns. The small printing house is the oldest in the nation west of the Rockies.

NATIONAL CEMETERY OF THE PACIFIC

2177 Puowaina Dr, 541-1430

This cemetery is the final resting place of many World War II, Korean War and Vietnam veterans. Ernie Pyle and the astronaut Ellison Onizuku are among the 26,000 buried there.

NEAL BLAISDELL CENTER

777 Ward Ave, 538-7331 or 527-5400

Within this 22-acre palm-studded center are a convention center, an exhibition hall and a theatre concert hall. There is always some event going on. The Honolulu Symphony is tops, and presents an exciting season of concerts. There is an opera season in the early spring. Check the local paper for current happenings in the Blaisdell Center.

NUUANI PALI

At the head of the Nuuani Valley is the dramatic 1200-foot pass where Kamehameha the Great defeated the Oahuans in a fierce battle in 1795. Thousands of the defeated warriors were forced over the precipice to meet death on the jagged rocks below. Take warm clothing when you visit the Pali, as it is very windy and cold. Some say the winds are the spirits of the dead. The view from this height is surely one of the world's greatest views.

PEARL HARBOR AND THE ARIZONA MEMORIAL
Highway 90, 423-1341

The memorial is administered by the National Park Service. There is a very informative visitor center you can stop in while waiting for the shuttle boat to the memorial. It is advisable to plan an early visit, due to the buildup of people waiting. Remember, the Park Service is the only tour on which you can actually visit the memorial. Nearby is the U.S.S. Bowfin, a World War II submarine which can be boarded for a visit.

QUEEN EMMA'S SUMMER PALACE
2913 Pali Highway, 595-3167

This white-pillared wooden Victorian-Hawaiian-style "palace" under large spreading trees in the Nuuanu Valley was the residence of Queen Emma during the hot summer months. The Daughters of Hawaii maintain the house and will answer your questions. There is a fine collection of Hawaiiana that includes Queen Emma's wedding gown.

ROYAL HAWAIIAN HOTEL
2259 Kalakaua Ave, 923-7311

To spend an evening in the Monarch Room, watching the moon over Waikiki Beach while listening to the Brothers Cazimero music is a special memory. The hotel, built in 1927, is a Honolulu treasure with its Spanish-Moorish design, beautiful grounds and grand lobby.

TAMASHIRO FISH MARKET
802 N King St, 841-8047

Do you like to look at live and wiggling sea creatures? Tamashiro has aisles, buckets and bins full of every imaginable fish, crabs, lobsters, oysters and things you have never seen. The bustling market is considered the best in Honolulu. Locals buy Poki, and if you have any questions about anything from the sea, Tamashiro knows the answers.

2-16-91
HONOLULU

U.S. ARMY MUSEUM AND BATTERY RANDOLPH
Ft. Derussy, Kalia Rd, 843-2639

The name of this museum may sound boring but inside is a fascinating history of military happenings in the Pacific. The battery was built to house 14-inch shore guns. When this fortification became obsolete, the Army tried to tear down the 22-foot walls. This proved to be to difficult an undertaking, so the Army wisely decided to make it a museum. The collection includes a Japanese mini-submarine, tanks, and a jeweled baton once owned by Herman Goering.

UNIVERSITY OF HAWAII
University Ave, Moana Valley, 948-8111

If you have time, a stroll around the 300-acre campus with its 500 varieties of tropical plants is very interesting. There is a Jean Charlot mural in the Administration building. The John F. Kennedy Theatre offers many excellent theatre and music events.

WAIKIKI AQUARIUM
2777 Kalakau Ave, 923-9741

There are over 300 species of fish in fifty-three tanks, and you can see the endangered Hawaiian monk seal. Guided tours and audio guides are available. The aquarium also offers guided day and evening walks along the shore and reef areas. Everyone will enjoy seeing the brightly-colored tropical fish.

HONOLULU
2·16·91
MARITIME MUSEUM

JOAN DOMINIS
HONOLULU
2-17-91

HONOLULU RESTAURANTS

Dining in Honolulu is a unique pleasure. There is absolutely the world's most amazing choice of restaurants. One may find every imaginable ethnic selection with a price variation that goes from a tiny price for a bowl of soup at a saimen stand to an expensive bill at a five-star restaurant. Honolulu is dense with familiar fast-food chains convenient for tourists, but for only a few dollars more you can dine overlooking the Pacific with caring service and a tropical atmosphere. Friday is Aloha day in Honolulu, when everyone dresses in Hawaiian-style clothes and the restaurants feature local cuisine.

AUNTIE PASTO'S
1099 S Beretania St, 523-8850

In spite of the casual appearance here, the food is very Italian and well cooked. The wine is served in tumblers and the portions are generous. There are lines for dinner, as this spot is very popular with locals. It is a convenient location for dining before events at the Blaisdell Center.

BAGWELLS
Hyatt Regency, 2424 Kalakaua Ave, 922-9292

This four-star restaurant offers impeccable service and food, for a fine dining evening. The wine list is impressive. Fresh opakapaka is prepared with Pacific-inspired sauces, and the duck breast with banana puree is outstanding. The room, with its tall windows above Kuhio Beach, is classy.

CANLIS
2100 Kalakaua Ave, 923-2324

There are lava walls, with waterfalls and orchids. Popular since its opening in 1947, Canlis has a deserved reputation for fresh fish and choice steaks.

COMPADRES MEXICAN BAR AND GRILL
Ward Center, upper level, 1200 Ala Moana Blvd, 523-1307

This is the a favorite Mexican restaurant in Honolulu. There are views of the water and an open-air lanai. The ceviche is made with fresh local fish, and the carne asada and chicken mole are outstanding. Margaritas made with peach, banana and strawberry are popular. Compadres is a fun place.

GARDEN CAFE
Honolulu Academy of Arts, 900 S Beretania, 531-8865

A visit to this outstanding art museum with its famous art collection is a must. To add to the exciting experience, plan to dine at the Garden Cafe. The food is outstanding and the whole operation is run by volunteers. They are dedicated and do a first-rate job. Lunch is served Tuesday through Friday, but reservations are necessary for this delightful treat.

GOLDEN DRAGON

Hilton Hawaiian Village, Rainbow Tower, 2005 Kalia Rd, 949-4321

If you are searching for very special Cantonese dining, this is the place. There is a long menu filled with delights served in a lovely dining room. Do make reservations, as the Golden Dragon fills up fast. If you are a tea connoisseur, you will enjoy their selection.

GREEK ISLAND TAVERNA

2570 S Beretania St, 943-0052

The Taverna has been making authentic and tasty Greek food since 1983. It is as good as any food in Greece. All the traditional dishes such as souvlaki, mousaka, and dolmas are made fresh and wonderful. Sometimes there is Greek music, and while you don't come to Honolulu to find a Greek evening, this will break up the occasional overkill of Polynesian things.

HAU TREE LANAI

New Otani Beach Hotel, 2863 Kalakaua Ave, 923-1555

Under woven branches of twin Hau trees right on the beach, this is unrivaled atmosphere. Robert Louis Stevenson enjoyed sitting under these trees. This is a spot for a memorable relaxed breakfast or a sunset dinner.

HELENA'S HAWAIIAN FOODS

1364 N King St, 845-8044

This tiny local dining spot has been in business since 1946. This is the place to find real Hawaiian food like poi, lomi, poke and haupia. Kalua pig will be packed for you to take back to the mainland. This is a no fuss or frills place with caring friendly owners.

HOUSE WITHOUT A KEY

Halekulani Hotel, 2199 Kalia Rd, 923-2311

If you want an everlasting memory, make plans to be at the terrace of the House Without a Key at sunset. The panoramic view of ocean and Diamond Head is unsurpassed. There are always top music groups playing for you entertainment. Sometimes they include "Miss Hawaii," who performs classical hula and songs. The tantalizing light food includes coconut shrimp with a plum sauce, and a fabulous Hawaiian salad with Maui onions and Kula tomatoes. The Halekulani coconut cake is legendary. This is also one of the greatest spots for a lovely buffet breakfast.

JOHN DOMINIS
43 Ahui St, off Ala Moana Blvd, 523-0955

The approach to John Dominis is on a road which is part of the commercial fishing industry of the Kewalo Basin, and you do wonder what a fine restaurant is doing in this neighborhood! It's there because of the view of this historic piece of waterfront. You can watch surfing, boats and the changing moods of the ocean. The terraced rooms, with koi and other exotic sea creatures drifting through a winding stream, add to the dramatic atmosphere. The list of fresh fish is one of the largest offered, and can be prepared in your favorite style. The curries and duck are outstanding and so is the wine list. Reservations are necessary, as over 50% of the customers are local. This is the spot for a big splurge or to make an impression on a sweetheart.

ROYAL HAWAIIAN
2·16·91

KEO'S THAI CUISINE
625 Kapahulu Ave, 737-8240 (also in Ward Center)

Keo's is everybody's favorite place for Thai cuisine. It is the spot to see movie stars and enjoy the spicy creative cooking. The curries, with their coconut milk sauce, are tops, and the spring rolls are delicious. This is a restaurant that has orchids coming out of every nook and cranny. If you're a devotee of Thai food, this is not to be missed. Kapahulu is on the outskirts of Waikiki, but can be an interesting walk or short cab ride.

KING TSIN
McCully St, 946-3273

If you're looking for good Szechuan food, this is your place. The hot and sour soup is perfectly made. There is a big menu that includes all kinds of Chinese favorites, and take-out service is available.

LA MER
Halekulani Hotel, 2199 Kalia Rd, 923-2311

This is a premier five-star restaurant. It is French, but with Hawaiian overtones to the food. Tall windows overlook the sea and there is a refined intimacy to the dining room. La Mer is the choice for a special occasion. The prices are no higher than in any other city's fine restaurants. The menu offers a *prix fixe* as well as a la carte dining.

MICHEL'S
Colony Surf Hotel, 3895 Kalakaua Ave, 923-6552

Sit overlooking Sans Souci Beach, so close you feel you can touch it. This restaurant is a favorite for sunset dining and Sunday brunch. Everything is served with class, and only the finest ingredients are used.

MONARCH ROOM
Royal Hawaiian Hotel, 2259 Kalakaua Ave, 923-7311

Famous for its dinner shows, this is an ornate large room overlooking the beach at Waikiki. It was originally called The Persian Room. The famous Brothers Cazimero perform here and are a show not to be missed. The food is excellent and includes traditional and local favorites. Call for reservations and performance schedules.

PATTI'S CHINESE KITCHEN
Makai Market, Ala Moana Center, 1450 Ala Moana Blvd

If you ask local residents where they like to go for Chinese food, many will say Patti's. It is fun dining in this huge food hall, where every kind of food is available. It is self-service; you fill your tray and find a seat. Patti's is the ultimate in a sort of Chinese cafeteria. There is a chance to see how each dish looks, and whatever you select, it will be fresh and wonderful.

PERRY'S SMORGY RESTAURANTS
various locations in Honolulu.

These buffet restaurants offer excellent value for breakfast, lunch or dinner. You can come back for seconds from a large selection of quite well-cooked food. Kona coffee is served, and the fresh Island fruits are outstanding. If you pick the location at the Outrigger Waikiki Hotel, you can have an ocean view.

ROY'S
6600 Kalanianaole Highway, 396-7697 (open for dinner only)

Roy Yamaguchi, one of America's celebrated chefs, opened this restaurant in 1988. It has been filled with admiring followers ever since. His cooking combines the best of East and West, with a special Hawaiian feeling. The view of the Pacific between Koko and Diamond Head is exciting, and each menu item provides a real dining adventure. The restaurant is located in the Kai suburb. It is always crowded with locals, so be sure to make reservations.

RAINBOW LANAI
Hilton Hawaiian Village, 949-4321

The special blend of Hawaiian and Pacific flavors at the Rainbow Lanai is outstanding. You can sit at a table with an ocean view and dine on fresh Ahi (tuna) with lime juice, or opakapaka with a fresh basil sauce. There is a Hawaiian dinner buffet each night. The satay appetizer is delicious, and the special coconut cake will melt in your mouth. This is a popular spot for breakfast. The Lanai offers a special children's menu.

SHORE BIRD BEACH BROILER
Outrigger Reef Hotel, 2169 Kalia Rd, 922-2877

You will find, inside the free Honolulu tourist guide booklets, coupons for discounts at the Shore Bird. Use them! This is a great happy place to be, right on the beach. The breakfast buffet is generous and quite good. Dinner is action time, when you select your main dish and cook it over a long charcoal broiler. There is a salad bar and lots of rather loud music.

SURF ROOM
Royal Hawaiian Hotel, 2259 Kalakaua Ave, 923-7311

This is casual dining with fabulous views, right on the beach, a wonderful spot for light dining with Waikiki atmosphere.

TAHITIAN LANAI
Waikikian Hotel, 1811 Ala Moana Blvd, 946-6541

Dining under thatched huts with a Polynesian-Hawaiian style menu in a sort of Forties setting. Doves nibble your muffin crumbs and life seems to slow down. We hope this can stay nestled among the highrises forever. This is a really perfect place for breakfast.

T.G.I FRIDAY'S
950 Ward Ave, 523-5841

This is part of a mainland restaurant chain, but somehow works very well in Honolulu. The food and menu are fun. There is always a lively crowd and the location is convenient.

THE WILLOWS
901 Hausten St, 946-4808

The Willows is a place to experience a real Old Honolulu dining experience. There is the thatched-roof atmosphere with koi ponds, and the famous Thursday poi lunch. This is a unique experience where diners relax and enjoy a special impromptu stage show. Performers volunteer from the audience. They can range from the local Safeway manager doing a hula, to a famous Broadway star singing the Hawaiian Love Song. This is a place where you can have traditional Hawaiian foods as well as fresh fish, curries and Chinese favorites.

WINDOWS OF HAWAII
1441 Ala Moana Blvd, 941-9138

The restaurant looks like a sort of flying saucer on top of the Ala Moana Building. It is actually 400 feet in the sky, and revolves once an hour to give a panoramic view of the city. The food is satisfactory, and the service good. If you like sky views, don't miss this.

WO FAT
115 N Hotel St, 533-6393

This 1882 landmark is a curious sight. Dine upstairs with a dragon mural and a big Cantonese menu. Many Chinatown tours end with lunch at Wo Fat.

HOTELS

There are over 25,000 hotel rooms in Honolulu, most of them in the Waikiki area. This is certainly where the action is, and the place to be. Many travel packages for Honolulu include hotels with air fares and can be quite remarkable bargains. This list includes only the more famous and popular; there are many more in the city.

COLONY SURF
2895 Kalakaua Ave, 923-5751

This is run like a small European hotel, and has one- and two-room suites. The location, away from the Waikiki crowds, is quiet, with a lovely beach in front of the hotel. An added attraction is Michel's award-winning restaurant.

HALEKULANI
2199 Kalia Rd, 923-2311

Elegant, with perfect taste in everything, the Halekulani is a favorite. You can see the beach from nearly all of the rooms. The hotel contains three outstanding restaurants: Orchids, La Mer, and House Without a Key.

HILTON HAWAIIAN VILLAGE
2005 Kalia Rd, 949-4321

This is the largest hotel along the beach and is like an entire village. There are shops, shows, dining and special events. If you are visiting with a family, there are enough activities to keep everyone entertained.

HYATT REGENCY WAIKIKI
2424 Kalakaua Ave, 922-9292

The two 39-story towers, around an atrium with waterfalls, are as dramatic as the views from these hotel rooms. Kuhio Beach, across the street, is one of the best spots for sunning and swimming.

OUTRIGGER REEF
2169 Kalia Rd, 923-3111

This is one of the more reasonable hotels on the ocean. The Outrigger hotels throughout Honolulu offer much for the budget traveler. They are well-run and many have kitchenettes.

SURFRIDER MOANA HOTEL
2365 Kalakaua Ave, 922-3111

This hotel, the first on Waikiki Beach, has been welcoming guests since 1901. Today, historically renovated, it is a stunning hotel that retains the mood of the past. The Banyan Tree Bar, under the century-old banyan tree where Robert Louis Stevenson liked to sit, is a favorite meeting place.

PRINCESS KAIULANI HOTEL
120 Kaiulani Ave, 922-5811

The Princess is convenient, with moderate prices. There are restaurants and a Polynesian show room.

ROYAL HAWAIIAN HOTEL
2259 Kalakaua Ave, 923-7311

Known worldwide as "the pink palace of the Pacific," this lovely hotel was built in 1927 by the Matson Navigation Company for their passengers sailing to Honolulu. All the rich and famous have spent time here. It takes three people three hours each day to make the orchid "stems" of the Radiant Flower Tree at the entrance to the Monarch Room. Even if you are not staying here, enjoy dining in one of the excellent restaurants, or a drink at the Mai Tai bar.

INDEX

HAU TREE GANG
HONOLULU

BIOGRAPHY

Betty Evans was born in Pasadena, California, and is a third-generation Californian. Betty now lives in Hermosa Beach, California, where she is a cooking teacher and food editor of the South Bay EASY READER. In addition to her food interests, she is an honorary docent at the Los Angeles Museum of Natural History, Civic Beautification chairman for the Hermosa Garden Club, and California Collection chairman for the Hermosa Beach Friends of the Library. She is a past Hermosa Beach "Woman of the Year."

Her family, who help in testing recipes, include artist husband Gordon, son Bob (an underwater photographer and inventor living in Santa Barbara), daughter Suzanne (an artist and chef in Zurich), and daughter Jean Evans Rosen, a singer and stationery designer in Quartz Hill, California.

HONOLULU COOKING is the latest in a popular series that includes "San Francisco Cooking with Betty Evans", "London Cooking with Betty Evans", "Rome Cooking with Betty Evans", "Paris Cooking with Betty Evans", "Venice Cooking with Betty Evans", and "California Cooking with Betty Evans". Betty is currently working on *California Wine Country Cooking.*

9E
2-17-91
HONOLULU

Betty and Joan making leis, 1980

Gordan and Hal, Barber's Point, 1980

Gordon and Betty, 1991, The Willows

HONOLULU 7·2·90

Mail Order Information

For additional copies of COOKING WITH BETTY EVANS books send $6.95 per book plus $1.50 for shipping and handling. In California add 6 3/4% sales tax. Make checks payable to Betty Evans, 1769 Valley Park Avenue, Hermosa Beach, California 90254, Telephone (213) 379-5932.

☐ CALIFORNIA COOKING WITH BETTY EVANS $6.95

☐ VENICE COOKING WITH BETTY EVANS $6.95

☐ PARIS COOKING WITH BETTY EVANS $6.95

☐ ROME COOKING WITH BETTY EVANS $6.95

☐ LONDON COOKING WITH BETTY EVANS $6.95

☐ SAN FRANCISCO COOKING WITH BETTY EVANS $6.95

☐ HONOLULU COOKING WITH BETTY EVANS $6.95

Also available through local bookstores that use R.R. Bowker Company BOOKS IN PRINT catalogue system. Order through publisher SUNFLOWER INK for bookstore discount.

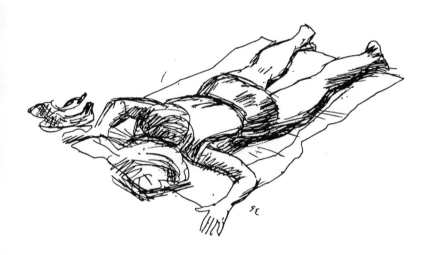